ELLIOT CARTER

EIGHT PIECES

for Four Timpani (one player)

CONTENTS

AMP-6820

1995 Printing

ISBN 978-0-7935-4848-4

Associated Music Publishers, Inc.

DISTRIBUTED BY

HAL•LEONARD®
CORPORATION

7777 W. BLUEMOUND RD. P.O. BOX 13819 MILWAUKEE, WI 53213

Performance Notes

1. *Public performance:* The printing order of these eight pieces was chosen largely to facilitate page turns, hence this order is not meant to suggest the order of performance. The group of eight is a collection of pieces from which not more than four are ever to be played as a suite in public. The order of these should be chosen to produce the maximum of variety, possibly according to the following suggestions:
   (a) If pedal timpani are available, III and/or VI may be included.
   (b) IV, V, VII and VIII can be used as beginning or ending pieces, while I, II, III and VI can be performed between them.
   (c) When played in sequence, it is important that not more than one pitch be carried over from one piece to the next — hence some may be transposed.

2. *Timpani:* Although all eight pieces can be performed on four standardized drums — 30″, 28″, 25″ and 23″ — other sized drums can be used to favor the effect of certain pieces. Although pedal timpani are required for III and VI, their use is not essential for the other pieces. However, pedal timpani can be useful for quick tuning changes between pieces for public performance.

3. *Sticks:* Sticks for I, III, IV, V and VII should be chosen to bring out the character of each piece. In VIII, medium-hard sticks are suggested; in VI, wooden snare drum sticks. In II, special rattan sticks with cloth (corduroy)-covered tips produce the best effect (see Example 1). IV uses a soft bass drum stick for its final note. I and VIII call for the reversing of the timpani sticks to strike with the wooden handles or butts. The striking with the wood is indicated
   BUTT , and the usual way of striking is indicated HEAD

4. *Stick strokes:* Unless otherwise specified, the usual type of stroke is to be used. This "normal stroke" is indicated by the sign NS when used to cancel the "dead stroke" DS — as in II, IV, and at the end of I. A "dead stroke" is one in which the head of the stick is held down on the drum after striking to damp all resonance at once.
   The appearance of the small sign ⌀ , found in all of the pieces except VI, indicates *hand damping.*
   In VI, the sign ⤬ means *on the rim* (not on the drum head), and the sign ⊗ means *rim shot.*

5. *Striking positions on the drum head:* To produce a wide variety of different sound qualities, various striking positions are suggested. They are notated as follows:

   Ⓝ———————┐   Normal striking position on head
   Ⓒ———————┐   Striking at center of head
   Ⓡ———————┐   Striking on head very near the rim
       (see Example 2)
   Ⓝ - - - - - ⇥Ⓒ   Change gradually from normal position to center of head

   Each of these positions should produce a distinctly different sound. Where nothing is suggested, the choice of striking positions is left to the discretion of the player.

6. *Special effects:*
   II: In the use of the cloth-covered rattan sticks, two types of striking are indicated (see Example 1):

   Tp   Striking with the tip
   Hd   Striking with the head

II: *Articulation* — The various degrees of accentuation in II should be clearly audible:
    (a) slight accents at the beginning of each measure;
    (b) lighter accents at the beginning of each beamed group within the measure;
    (c) still lighter accents at the beginning of inner beams of sixteenth notes.
The sign / indicates an accent as at the beginning of a measure.
The sign ∪ weakens the above indications.

III: Harmonics sounding an octave above the tuned pitch of the drum may be produced by pressing one or two fingers on the head of the drum half-way between the rim and center, and striking near the rim. The harmonic is notated ◇

III: *Sympathetic resonance* (called for on page 8, line 3, and page 9, line 1) — The pitch played on the drum notated on the large staff is meant to produce a sympathetic resonance in the drum notated on the small staff below. If this does not occur effectively, with a vibration loud enough to make the small-note glissandi audible, then the drums indicated in small notes should be struck softly at the same time or immediately after the other drums.

VI: The 'sneak entrances' should be soft enough to be covered up by the ring of the previous loud notes.

Example 1   Cloth-covered Rattan Stick

Tp ——(tip)—>
single layer
of cloth
over tip

Hd   (head)
two or three layers
of cloth on sides

Example 2   Striking Positions on Drum Head

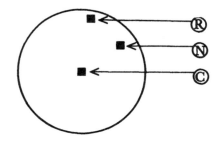

Ⓡ   As close as possible to rim, still sounding pitch

Ⓝ   Normal striking position

Ⓒ   Center of drum head

EIGHT PIECES
for Four Timpani
(one player)

to Al Howard

I. Saëta

Elliott Carter

* See Performance Note #4 regarding damping notation.

6

1950/1966

to Paul Price

II. Moto Perpetuo*

Elliott Carter

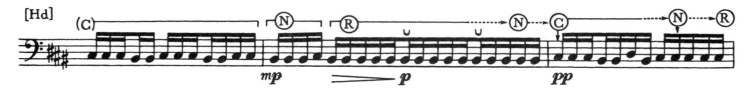

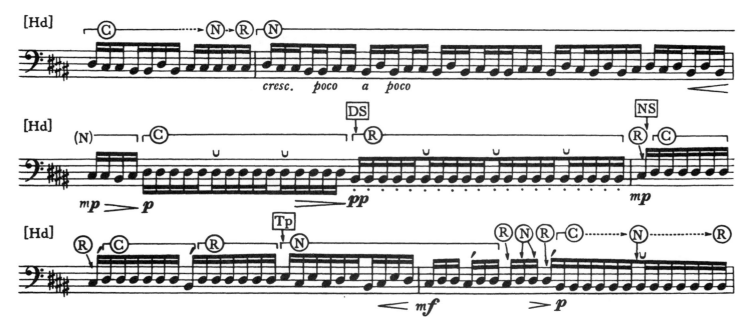

* See Performance Note #6 regarding accents and sticks.

8

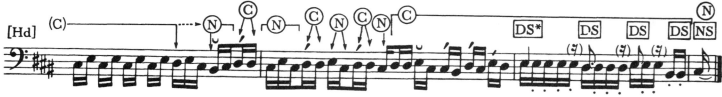

* With the stick of one hand, strike and hold against drum head; the other stick plays the repeated notes.

1950/1966

to Jan Williams

III. Adagio

Elliott Carter

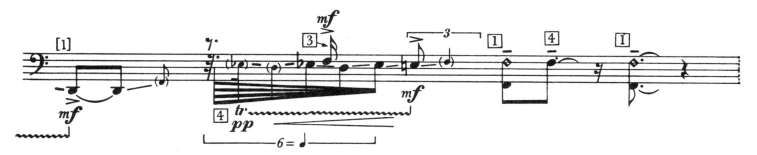

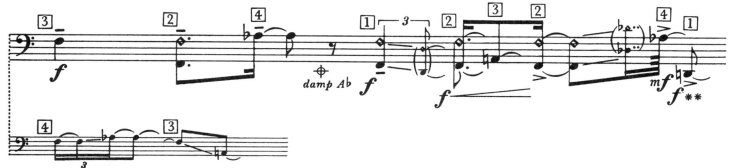

sympathetic resonance (see Performance Note #6)

* If this piece is performed after another of the series, it is only necessary to tune Drum 3. Drums 1, 2 and 4 may start on any note and slide into the first notes not in parentheses.

** The drums played before the harmonic and glissando note should be loud enough to form a ringing background without covering that note. (See Performance Note #6 regarding the production of harmonics.)

sympathetic resonance (see Performance Note)

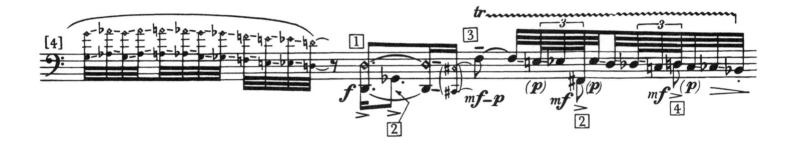

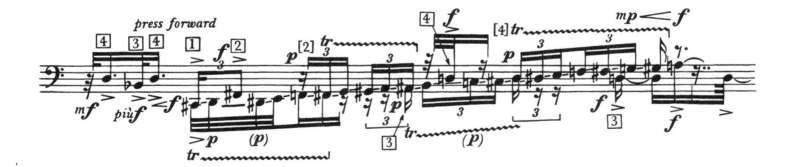

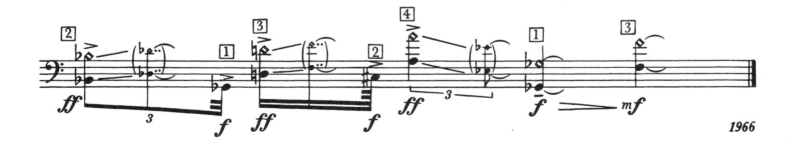

1966

to Morris Lang

IV. Recitative

Elliott Carter

Adagio drammatico (♩=49)

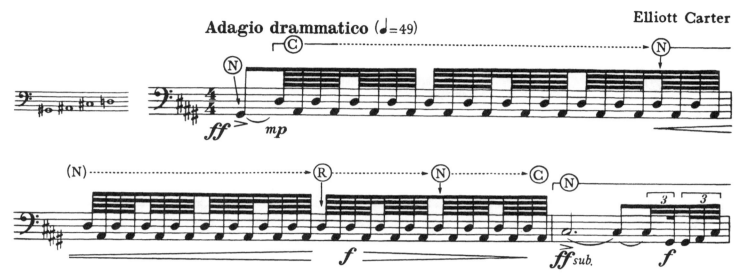

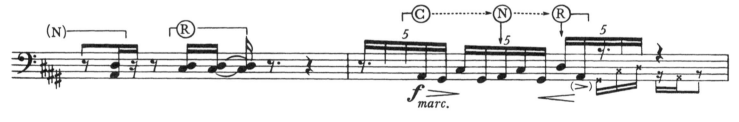

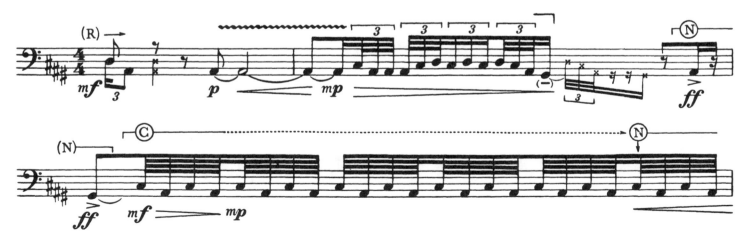

*All rests in IV and V indicate hand damping.

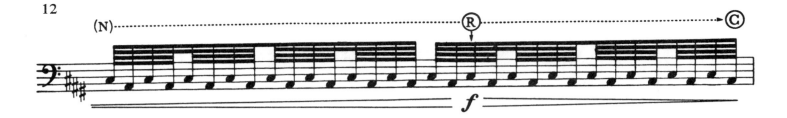

1950/1966

to Paul Price

V. Improvisation

Elliott Carter

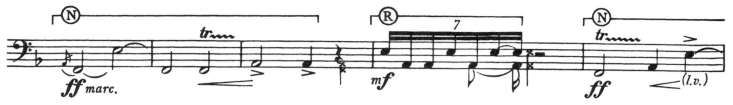

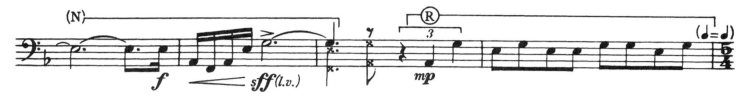

* Let each tone fade out without striking again.

1950/1966

to Jan Williams

VI. Canto

Elliott Carter

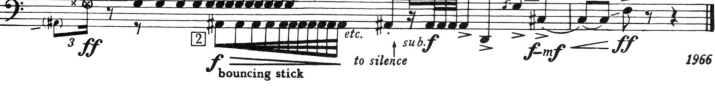

1966

to Raymond DesRoches

VII. Canaries

Elliott Carter

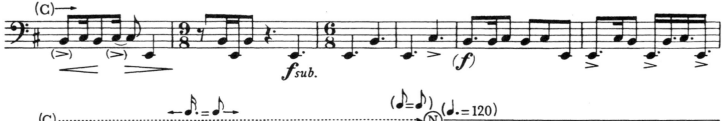

1950/1966

to Saul Goodman

VIII. March

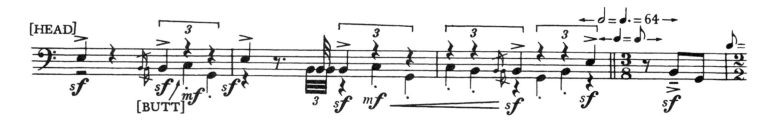

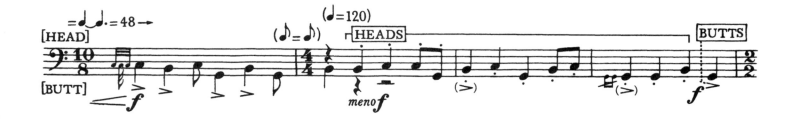

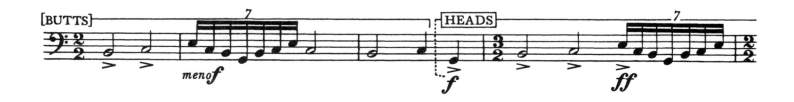

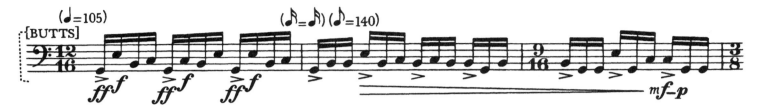

1950/1966